JESUS,
YOU TAKE OVER

Prayers for Surrender to God's Will for Private Devotion

A Prayer of the Servant of God
Fr. Dolindo Ruotolo

St. Jerome Library

WWW.STJEROMELIBRARY.ORG

About Fr. Dolindo Ruotolo (October 6,1882AD-Noember 19, 1970AD) Napoli, Italy:

Fr. Dolindo Ruotolo was born, in Naples, Italy on October 6,1882AD. Ordained at the young age of 23 on June 24, 1905AD, he dedicated every moment of his long life to prayer and penance at the service of the thousands of faithful who asked for his spiritual direction and turned to him for help and comfort. Don Dolindo Ruotolo is the author of a profound and huge Commentary on the Holy Scripture in 33 volumes. Besides that, he left a very large number of theological, ascetical and mystical writings. He also answered thousands of letters. He wrote also thousands of notes on holy images to offer spiritual direction to people. Don Dolindo had a keen understanding of the human soul and thus he was always able to help people to see the light of God. Forever at work, tireless in helping souls, in the midst of unspeakable suffering of every kind, as victim soul for mankind, he was sustained by a wonderful freshness of spirit that transformed his life into a hymn to life. Paralyzed for the last ten years of his life, Don Dolindo Ruotolo died in Naples on November 19, 1970AD, in the extreme voluntary poverty he had lived all his life. His body lies in the Church where he served as Pastor, Our Lady of Lourdes and St. Joseph of the Aged, whee now, more than ever, people flock to him and seek out his tomb, confident of his intercession.

Fr. Ruotolo referred to himself as "the Madonna's little old man."

Padre Pio said to Fr. Ruotolo, "The whole of paradise is in your soul." And when pilgrims from Naples came to visit Padre Pio, he said, "Why do you come here, if you have Don Dolindo in Naples? Go to him, he's a saint!"

Fr. Ruotolo's body rests in his Parish Church Our Lady of Lourdes and St. Joseph of the Aged, Via Salvatore Tommasi, Napoli, Italy.

JESUS, YOU TAKE OVER!

A prayer of the Servant of God,
Fr. Dolindo Ruotolo

Jesus to the soul:

Why are you upset and agitated?
Leave your cares to Me and all will
be fine. I tell you honestly, every act
of true and blind reliance on Me,

results in what you desire and will resolve all your difficulties.

Abandonment in Me does not mean being frustrated, becoming anxious and desperate, offering Me your anxious prayer, that I may follow you and have your anxiety be a prayer.

Abandonment means to shut the eyes of your soul in peace, moving your thoughts away from your troubles, and instead of thinking about your worries and pain, let Me take over your troubles. Simply say: **Jesus, You take over.** To be worried, restless, and to think of the consequences of an event is the opposite of reliance, it is really contrary to it.

It is like a child, who wants his mom to take care his needs, but in the way he wants: and with his whims and childish ideas he hampers her work. Shut your eyes and go with the flow of My grace. Do not ponder over your present moment and put away thoughts of your future as a temptation; rest in Me, believe in My goodness and I swear on My Love, that if you think like this: **Jesus, You take over,** I indeed will do it for you, I will comfort you, free you, and guide you. If I have to take you in a different direction from the one you are looking at, I will train you, I pick you up in my arms, and you will find yourself, like a baby sleeping in his mother's arms, on the other shore. What gives you immense stress and hurts you, is your reasoning over it, your thoughts and the pains it gives you; it is wanting at all costs to take care by yourself of what is afflicting you.

How many things I can do, be it a material or a spiritual need, when the soul turns to Me, looks at Me and says to Me: **Jesus, You take over**, and close its eyes and rests in Me! You do not receive many graces because you insist on getting them by yourself; but instead, you will receive numberless graces, when your prayer is in full reliance on Me. When you are in pain, and you pray that I may act, you want Me to act as you believe I should... you do not turn to Me; instead, you want Me to submit to your ideas; you are like a sick person who does not ask the doctor for the cure, but tells him what the cure is to be. Don't be like this, but pray as I taught you in the Our Father: *Hallowed be Your Name*, which means, may You be glorified in this need of mine; *Your kingdom* *come*, which means, everything may work toward Your Kingdom in us and in the world; *Your will be done on earth as it is in heaven*, which means, You direct it as it seems best to You

for the good of our eternal and temporal life.

When you truly tell me: Your will be done, which is the same then to say: **Jesus, You take over**, then I do intervene with all My omnipotence, and I will resolve every situation, even if there is no way out. For example, do you see your sickness becoming worse instead of improving? Don't become anxious, close your eyes and tell Me with

trust: Your will be done, **Jesus, You take over.** I repeat it, I do take care, I intervene like a doctor, and even do a miracle if it is necessary.

Does a patient become worse? Don't be frightened, close your eyes and say: **Jesus, You take over**. I tell you again: I will indeed do it for you, and there is no medicine more powerful than my loving intervention. I take over only when you close your eyes. You never sleep, you want to appraise everything, to think, to delve into everything; you choose to rely on human power, or, worse, on men, trusting their intervention. This is what hampers My words and My will. Oh, how much I long for this reliance in order to assist you, and how much I grieve to see your anxiety. Satan does just this: he gives you anxiety to remove Me from you and throw you into human initiative. Trust only in Me instead, rest in Me, rely on Me in everything. I do miracles in proportion to your complete reliance on Me, with no thought of yourself. I spread treasures of graces when you are in the most squalid poverty. If you have your own resources, even a few, or if you seek them, you are at the natural level, thus you follow the natural way of things, which often are dominated by Satan. Never a thinker or a philosopher has done any miracle, not even among the Saints; only he who relies on God does divine work. When you see that things become complicated, say with your eyes closed: *Jesus, I abandon myself to You*; **Jesus, You take over**, and stop worrying about it, because your mind is dull and for you it is difficult to distinguish evil; but trust in Me, and let your mind wander away from your thoughts. Do this for all your needs; all of you, do this, and you shall see great things, endless and silent miracles. I swear it on My Love. I shall indeed take over, you can be sure of it. Pray always with this loving confidence  and you shall have great peace and great fruits, even when I choose for you the grace of immolating yourself for reparation and the love that entails suffering. Do you believe it is impossible? Shut your eyes and say with all your soul: **Jesus, You take over.** Don't be

afraid, I indeed will take care of you, and you shall bless My Name, in humility. A thousand prayers do not equal only one act of abandonment; don't ever forget it. There is no better novena than this: *Oh Jesus I abandon myself to You*, **Jesus, You take over.**

The Surrender Novena

Daily Prayer

Why do you confuse yourselves by worrying? Leave the care of your affairs to Me and everything will be peaceful. I say to you in truth that every act of true, blind, complete surrender to me produces the effect that you desire and resolves all difficult situations.

O Jesus, I surrender myself to you, take care of everything!
(10 times)

Concluding Prayer

Mother, I am Yours now and forever. Through You and with You I always want to belong completely to Jesus.

Daily Prayer

Surrender to Me does not mean to fret, to be upset, or to lose hope, nor does it mean offering to Me a worried prayer asking Me to follow you and change your worry into prayer. It is against this surrender, deeply against it, to worry, to be nervous and to desire to think about the consequences of anything.

It is like the confusion that children feel when they ask their mother to see to their needs, and then try to take care of those needs for themselves so that their childlike efforts get in their mother's way. Surrender means to placidly close the eyes of the soul, to turn away from thoughts of tribulation and to put yourself in My care, so that only I act, saying, "You take care of it".

O Jesus, I surrender myself to you, take care of everything!
(10 times)

Concluding Prayer

Mother, I am Yours now and forever. Through You and

with You I always want to belong completely to Jesus.

Daily Prayer

How many things I do when the soul, in so much spiritual and material need, turns to me, looks at me and says to me; "You take care of it", then closes it's eyes and rests. In pain you pray for Me to act, but that I act in the way you want. You do not turn to Me, instead, you want me to adapt your ideas. You are not sick people who ask the doctor to cure you, but rather sick people who tell the doctor how to. So do not act this way, but pray as I taught you in the Our Father: "Hallowed be thy Name", that is, be glorified in my need.

"Thy kingdom come", that is, let all that is in us and in the world be in accord with Your kingdom. "Thy will be done on Earth as it is in Heaven", that is, in our need, decide as You see fit for our temporal and eternal life. If you say to Me truly: "Thy will be done", which is the same as saying: "You take care of it", I will intervene with all My omnipotence, and I will resolve the most difficult situations.

O Jesus, I surrender myself to you, take care of everything!
(10 times)

Concluding Prayer

Mother, I am Yours now and forever. Through You and with You I always want to belong completely to Jesus.

Day 4 Prayer

Daily Prayer

You see evil growing instead of weakening? Do not worry. Close your eyes and say to Me with faith: "Thy will be done, You take care of it". I say to you that I will take care of it, and that I will intervene as does a doctor, and I will accomplish miracles when they are needed. Do you see that the sick person is getting worse? Do not be upset, but close your eyes and say "You take care of it". I say to you that I will take care of it, and that there is no medicine more powerful than My loving intervention. By My love, I promise this to you.

O Jesus, I surrender myself to you, take care of everything!
(10 times)

Concluding Prayer

Mother, I am Yours now and forever. Through You and with You I always want to belong completely to Jesus.

DAY 5 PRAYER

Daily Prayer

And when I must lead you on
a path different from the one
you see, I will prepare you; I
will carry you in My Arms; I
will let you find yourself, like
children who have fallen

asleep in their mother's arms, on the other bank of the river. What troubles you and hurts you immensely are your reason, your thoughts and worry, and your desire at all costs to deal with what afflicts you.

O Jesus, I surrender myself to you, take care of everything!
(10 times)

Concluding Prayer

Mother, I am Yours now and forever. Through You and with You I always want to belong completely to Jesus.

Day 6 Prayer

Daily Prayer

You are sleepless; you want to judge everything, direct everything and see to everything and you surrender to human strength, or worse - to men themselves, trusting in their intervention, - this is what hinders My words and My views. Oh, how much I wish from you this surrender, to help you; and how I suffer when I see you so agitated! Satan tries to do exactly this: to agitate you and to remove you from My protection and to throw you into the jaws of human initiative. So, trust only in Me, rest in Me, surrender to Me in everything.

O Jesus, I surrender myself to you, take care of everything!
(10 times)

Concluding Prayer

Mother, I am Yours now and forever. Through You and with You I always want to belong completely to Jesus.

Day 7 Prayer

Daily Prayer

I perform miracles in proportion to your full surrender to Me and to your not thinking of yourselves. I sow treasure troves of graces when you are in the deepest poverty. No person of reason, no thinker, has ever performed miracles, not even among the saints. He does divine works whosoever surrenders to God. So don't think about it anymore, because your mind is dull and for you it is very hard to see evil and to trust in Me and to not think of yourself. Do this for all your needs, do this all of you and you will see great continual silent miracles. I will take care of things. I promise this to you.

O Jesus, I surrender myself to you, take care of everything!
(10 times)

Concluding Prayer

Mother, I am Yours now and forever. Through You and with You I always want to belong completely to Jesus.

DAY 8 PRAYER

Daily Prayer

Close your eyes and let yourself be carried away on the flowing current of My grace; close your eyes and do not think of the present, turning your thoughts away from the future just as you would from temptation. Repose in Me, believing in My goodness, and I promise you by My love that if you say "You take care of it," I will take care of it all; I will console you, liberate you and guide you.

O Jesus, I surrender myself to you, take care of everything!
(10 times)

Concluding Prayer

Mother, I am Yours now and forever. Through You and with You I always want to belong completely to Jesus.

Day 9 Prayer

Daily Prayer

Pray always in readiness to surrender, and you will receive from it great peace and great rewards, even when I confer on you the grace of immolation, of repentance and of love. Then what does suffering matter? It seems impossible to you? Close your eyes and say with all your soul, "Jesus, you take care of it". Do not be afraid, I will take care of things and you will bless My Name by humbling yourself. A thousand prayers cannot equal one single act of surrender, remember this well. There is no novena more effective than this.

O Jesus, I surrender myself to you, take care of everything!
(10 times)

Concluding Prayer

Mother, I am Yours now and forever. Through You and with You I always want to belong completely to Jesus.

THE ROSARY OF ABANDONMENT

God, come to my assistance.
Lord, make haste to help me.
Glory be.
Our Father.
Hail Mary.

1st Decade: **Jesus, You take over!**
(10 times on the beads of the Hail Mary).
Glory be.

2nd Decade: **Mother Mary, guide me.**
(10 times on the beads of the Hail Mary).
Glory be.

3rd Decade: **Jesus, You take over!**
(10 times on the beads of the Hail Mary).
Glory be.

4th Decade: **Mother Mary, guide me.**
(10 times on the beads of the Hail Mary).
Glory be.

5th Decade: **Jesus, You take over!**
(10 times on the beads of the Hail Mary).
Glory be.

In conclusion:
Hail Holy Queen

Made in the USA
Las Vegas, NV
12 August 2024

93725660R00026